THE G.I. SERIES

Left: Soldiers of the 24th Infantry Division (Mechanised) set up a 120mm mortar. The 120mm mortar is replacing the World War Two vintage 4.2 inch mortar. The mortar has greater range than the 4.2 inch. Its crew of five can deliver indirect fire rounds at an enemy target up to 7,250 meters away. A combination of M113 Armored Personnel Carriers (APC) and Bradley Infantry Fighting Vehicles (IFV) are parked behind the position.

THE G. I. SERIES

THE ILLUSTRATED HISTORY OF THE AMERICAN SOLDIER, HIS UNIFORM AND HIS EQUIPMENT

The U.S. Army Today

From the End of the Cold War to the Present Day

Christopher J. Anderson

CHELSEA HOUSE PUBLISHERS
PHILADELPHIA

Library of Congress Cataloging-in-Publication Data
Anderson, Christopher J.
The U.S. Army today: from the end of the Cold War to the present day / Christopher J. Anderson.
    p.   cm.— (The G.I. Series)
Originally published: London: Greenhill Books; Mechanicsburg, PA: Stackpole Books, © 1997, in series: G.I. series; 8.
Includes index.
Summary: A history of recent missions of the United States Army in both war and peacetime operations and a description of its present-day uniforms and equipment.
ISBN 0-7910-5372-5 (hc)
1. United States. Army—History—20th century.
2. United States. Army—Uniforms.   3. United States. Army—Equipment.   [1.United States. Army— History—20th century.   2. United States. Army— Uniforms.   3. United States. Army—Equipment.]
I. Title. II. Series: G.I. series (Philadelphia, Pa.)
UC483.A83 1999
355.1'4' 09730904—dc21   99-13176
                              CIP

ACKNOWLEDGEMENTS
All of the photographs in this book are from the collections of the United States Army Public Affairs Department and *National Guard* Magazine. Captions are credited as Army Public Affairs (APA) and *National Guard* Magazine (NGM), at the end of each caption. The author would like to thank Mr. Robert Melhorn of the Army Public Affairs and the staff of *National Guard* Magazine for their help in obtaining the photographs.

Designed and edited by DAG Publications Ltd
Designed by David Gibbons
Layout by Anthony A. Evans
Printed in Hong Kong

THE U.S. ARMY TODAY: FROM THE END OF THE COLD WAR TO THE PRESENT DAY

On 9 November 1989 the Berlin Wall began to come down. This event symbolised the end of the Cold War. Unfortunately, the end of the Soviet threat has meant that the world has become increasingly unstable.

By 1989 Panama's General Manuel Noriega was indicted in the United States on drug charges. Ignoring the results of free elections, he established himself as dictator. Despite repeated attempts by the Bush administration to remove Noriega for trial in the United States, he remained in power and harassed the thousands of American soldiers and civilians who lived in Panama. On 16 December 1989 matters came to a head when Panamanian Defense Forces (PDF) killed a U.S. Marine officer on duty in Panama City. The next day, President Bush ordered the military to proceed with Operation Just Cause.

Prior planning and preparation had proved crucial as the Army quickly began to move men and material from installations across the United States. On the evening of 20 December, 27,081 well-equipped and highly trained Army personnel attacked specific targets simultaneously. The suddenness and decisiveness of the American attack quickly neutralised all opposition. By the morning of the 21st most of the military objectives had been secured.

On the evening of 2 August 1990, not long after the successful completion of Operation Just Cause, an Iraqi army of 100,000 soldiers crashed across the border of Kuwait. The Iraqis occupied the country and advanced to within five miles of the Saudi Arabian border. Seeing the threat to Saudi Arabia as imminent, President Bush directed elements of the 82nd Airborne Division to deploy to Saudi Arabia. Operation Desert Shield, the initial American deployment to Saudi Arabia, had begun.

Throughout the remainder of 1990, as President Bush recruited a coalition of thirty-one allied nations, United States forces continued to deploy to the Persian Gulf. It was hoped that this initial deployment would end the threat of an Iraqi advance into Saudi Arabia, and force Saddam Hussein to abandon Kuwait.

While America built up the strength of its armed forces in Saudi Arabia, Saddam Hussein began digging in. The Iraqi army was the fourth largest in the world, with a great deal of combat experience from its eight-year war with Iran. In addition, the Iraqis were well entrenched behind two belts of defences. It was estimated that Hussein had more than a half-million troops in Kuwait prior to the start of the ground war. Hussein promised that any attempt to oust Iraq from Kuwait would result in the 'Mother of all battles'.

The massive deployment of troops to the Gulf did not force Hussein to retreat from Kuwait. After all attempts at a peaceful solution of the worsening situation had failed, the coalition forces, commanded by General Norman Schwarzkopf, commenced a massive air campaign against Iraqi positions on 16 January 1991; Operation Desert Storm had begun. This air campaign crippled Hussein's communications infrastructure, softened enemy defensive positions, gathered crucial intelligence and assured air superiority. As the air campaign increased in intensity, Hussein launched a series of SCUD missile attacks on Israel and Saudi Arabia. He hoped that by forcing the Israelis to retaliate, he would break up the coalition. Army Air Defense units quickly countered this threat with their Patriot missiles. While Allied forces established air supremacy in the skies over Iraq and Kuwait General Schwarzkopf finalised his plans for the destruction of the Iraqi ground forces.

Marines conducted operations in front of Iraqi positions to convince them that the main coalition assault would be made against their well-prepared positions. With the eyes of Iraqi commanders riveted to the front, General Schwarzkopf began secretly to move the VII Corps and the XVIII Airborne Corps to the west, far past the Iraqi right flank. The air assault against Iraq continued until 24 February when General Schwarzkopf began his famous 'Hail Mary Plan'. This plan called for coalition forces to pin the enemy to its positions while mobile forces conducted a massive sweep around the right flank of the Iraqi army.

As Marine and Arab coalition forces began assaulting Iraqi positions around Kuwait City, the VII Corps, commanded by General Frederick M. Franks, began its advance into Iraq. This advance was so rapid that in many instances the weapons of surrendering Iraqi soldiers were confiscated and the prisoners were simply told to move south as the armoured columns continued forward. The advance went on throughout the day and into the evening. The soldiers were able to continue to attack enemy positions at night with the help of night-vision equipment. By the next morning, the VII Corps had forced Iraqi forces into a shrinking pocket around Kuwait city.

At the same time that the VII Corps was advancing north, the XVIII Airborne Corps, commanded by Lieutenant General Gary Luck, moved north into Iraq. The corps halted at the town of As-Salam, where it engaged and destroyed an Iraqi Infantry Division. Later that morning, in the largest helicopter lift in history, 400 U.S. Army helicopters transported 2000 soldiers of the 101st Airborne Division into Iraq. The XVIII Airborne Corps continued to advance north, blocking any Iraqi withdrawal to the west.

The final day of the ground war saw the continuation of the rapid advance and stunning success of the first two days. The VII Corps tanks mauled Iraqi formations, while helicopters of the XVIII Airborne Corps continued to devastate Iraqi columns headed north. By the end of that day, Kuwait City was liberated, and President Bush declared an end to offensive ground operations.

Using speed and overwhelming firepower, the Allied forces in the Gulf destroyed twenty-nine Iraqi divisions in only three days of ground combat. The American contribution was huge; more than 600,000 American personnel were deployed to the Persian Gulf; of those, 144 lost their lives.

As the American Army returned home from its victory in the Persian Gulf, it was immediately tasked with the continuation of its force reduction. By the end of 1992 the size of the Active Army had dropped from 930,000 to 640,000 soldiers. The strength reduction was immediately apparent in Europe where the VII Corps was based. In Germany the corps that had performed so magnificently in the Persian Gulf War was deactivated and cased its colours.

Due to the downsizing, the focus of the Army had shifted from forward deployment and global conflict to regional contingencies and force projection. For the first time in forty years, the military might of the United States would be based in the Continental United States (CONUS) and not in Europe. Increased emphasis would now be placed on rapid deployment to world hot spots. Improved weapons systems and advanced technologies such as the M1A1 Tank, Bradley Fighting Vehicle, UH-64 Apache Attack Helicopter, UH-60 Black Hawk Helicopter and Multiple Launch Rocket System (MLRS) would allow the Army to retain its hitting power, while maintaining its smaller size.

In January 1993, just three months after returning from hurricane relief duty in Florida, elements of the 10th Mountain Division (Light) were alerted for deployment to Somalia. The country had been in the grip of a civil war since the death of its long-time dictator, Maxamed Siyaad Barre, in 1991. As the war between rival Somali warlords worsened, anarchy reigned in the country. Humanitarian efforts to bring food and relief to the people of Somalia were repeatedly thwarted by Somali warlords. At the beginning of 1993 the decision was made to send in American soldiers to support Operation Restore Hope. The operation was designed to ensure that humanitarian relief to Somalia arrived safely in the hands of people who needed it most. The Army was also tasked with defusing the dangerous situation in the country by confiscating the weapons of the warring parties prior to turning the relief effort over to the United Nations. By March, more than 16,000 personnel were on the ground in Somalia, principally around the capital city of Mogadishu.

Shortly after deployment to Somalia, what had been intended as a humanitarian effort turned violent as tensions with the forces of Somali warlord Mohammed Farah Aideed escalated. There were repeated sniper attacks on U.S. soldiers and Marines, and one civilian defence department employee was killed by sniper fire.

On 5 June 1993, forces commanded by Aideed ambushed a force of Pakistani peace-keepers, killing twenty-three and wounding fifty-nine. The Army responded quickly, and during 11, 12 and 13 June, conducted operations designed to neutralise weapon caches and radio installations controlled by Aideed.

In September four American soldiers were killed when a remote-controlled mine was exploded under their HUMVEE and later that month three more soldiers were killed when their helicopter was shot down. In response to the situation, the Army sent armour and aviation assets of the 24th Infantry Division (Mechanised) to Somalia to strengthen the elements of the 10th Mountain Division and the 75th Ranger Regiment.

The operations against Somali strongholds continued into October. On 3 October a detachment of the 75th Ranger Regiment was alerted to prepare for another mission into Mogadishu. Reports were received that some of Aideed's senior leadership were meeting at a hotel in the city. The plan was to launch a two-pronged operation. The first portion would be an aerial assault by Rangers in two helicopters. These Rangers would secure the building and take prisoners. While the building was being secured, a convoy of HUMVEES would proceed to the hotel to transport any prisoners.

The first phase of the operation had been successfully completed by 4:00 p.m.. However, just as the convoy arrived to pick up the prisoners, word was received that elsewhere in the city a Black Hawk helicopter, part of a patrol of three helicopters, had been shot down. The Rangers immediately set out under intense small-arms fire to reach the scene of the crash and rescue any survivors. As the Rangers worked toward the wreckage, another Blackhawk was shot down. Two special forces soldiers, Master Sergeant Gary Gordon and Sergeant First Class Randall Shughart, in the third helicopter, returned to the second downed helicopter to cover the injured crew.

As soon as the Rangers reached the first crash site, they immediately began taking small arms and grenade fire. Realising that they were encircled, the Rangers took cover in the surrounding buildings to await reinforcements.

A company of the 14th Infantry Regiment, 24th Infantry Division, was dispatched in HUMVEES and trucks to relieve the Rangers. Almost immediately they were ambushed. Travelling in thin-skinned vehicles, they were forced to turn back for armour support. Meanwhile, another company of the 14th, riding in armoured personnel carriers, was able to battle its way to the first crash site. The last part of the rescue was conducted on foot to relieve the surrounded Rangers and their prisoners, despite the attacks of an estimated 1500 Somali. The fight to reach the Rangers was intense. Captain Michael Whetstone, the company commander, noted that each man fired more than 1000 rounds.

At the second crash site, Gordon and Shughart fought a running battle with Somali to protect Warrant Officer Michael Durant who, although wounded, had survived the crash. The two men set up a perimeter around the crash site, and were constantly patrolling the area to keep the Somali away from the wounded Durant. After they had expended all of their ammunition, the two men returned to the crash site to get more ammunition. Shughart was killed when his ammunition ran out and Gordon was killed later after handing a weapon with the last five rounds of ammunition in it to Durant. Durant was later captured by the Somali and spent eleven days as a prisoner.

Shortly after Durant's capture, the company of the 14th that had been originally forced back arrived at the crash site to retrieve the bodies. By the end of the day, eighteen American soldiers had been killed.

After the 3 October battle, hostilities ceased between U.N. forces and Aideed and the situation went into negotiation. By March of 1994, American forces were withdrawn from Somalia.

President Bill Clinton carried out the last act of Operation Restore Hope when he posthumously awarded the Medal of Honor to Gordon and Shughart for their actions on 3 October. These became the only Medals of Honor awarded since the conclusion of the Vietnam war.

While the Army looked at the lessons of Operation Restore Hope, President Clinton was becoming increasingly frustrated by the refusal of General Raul Cedras in Haiti to relinquish his control of the country to Jean-Bertrand Aristide, the first democratically elected leader of the country. President Clinton called on the 10th Mountain Division, Special Forces units and elements of the XVIII Airborne Corps to prepare for Operation Uphold Democracy. This operation called for the invasion of Haiti, if necessary, to restore Aristide to power.

Negotiations continued throughout September without result. The Army began moving on 17 September. However, during eleventh-hour negotiations, and faced with the imminent arrival of the 82nd Airborne Division, the Junta leaders backed down. What had been planned as a hostile invasion changed to a peaceful occupation. American soldiers of the XVIII Airborne Corps and other units landed in Haiti and secured the country for the return of Aristide.

Just as Operation Uphold Democracy was getting under way, Saddam Hussein began to mass troops on the Iraq-Kuwait border. This action provoked an immediate response by President Clinton who dispatched elements of the 24th Infantry Division to Saudi Arabia for Operation Vigilant Warrior, a show of strength and resolve. Hussein immediately backed down. While neither the operation in Haiti nor Kuwait had resulted in bloodshed, both demonstrated the power and rapid reaction abilities of the Army to respond to multiple crises around the world on short notice.

Somalia had not long been forgotten when the American public was confronted with even more horrible pictures coming out of former Yugoslavia. Here, warring ethnic factions had destroyed the stability of the country. Repeated attempts had been made by the international community and United Nations' negotiators to end the war. Pressure to do something mounted as evidence of 'ethnic cleansing' and other atrocities began to emerge from the bloodiest conflict to be fought in Europe since the end of World War Two.

By December 1995 the decision had been made to send American forces into Bosnia as part of a larger international force. Operation Joint Endeavor was designed to enforce a cease-fire that had been signed in November between the warring factions.

In December, American engineers bridged the Sava river and the heavy firepower of the 1st Armored Division travelled to Tuzla, where the American task force is headquartered. By March 1996, 17,750 G.I.s were operating in Bosnia. In order to demonstrate the strength of the task force, there were also 100 Abrams tanks, 240 Bradley Fighting Vehicles and 24 Apache Attack Helicopters. In a striking example of how the world has changed since the end of the Cold War, the Russians have a brigade of 1500 men who are working alongside American soldiers. Since the arrival of American soldiers, the warring factions have been separated in their zone of responsibility. The airport at Tuzla has been reopened, and troops have begun the dangerous process of removing thousands of mines that had been planted in the area during the war.

While the Army was deployed to Bosnia, it was completing the restructuring that had resulted in the smallest American army since Pearl Harbor. Since the end of the Cold War the Army has reduced its size by 500,000, taken all of its nuclear and chemical weapons out of its table of organisation and closed more than 600 bases around the world. Despite these drastic reductions in force, the operational tempo (OPTEMPO) of the army has increased by 300 per cent. Today the average American soldier spends 138 days a year away from his or her home. In order to meet the demands placed on the soldier by this vastly increased OPTEMPO, greater use will be made of advanced technologies such as those in systems like the M1A2 Abrams tank and the MLRS. Despite the many changes that the force has undergone since the end of the Cold War, the G.I. will continue to do what he has done since 1775 – fight his nation's wars.

FOR FURTHER READING

Soldiers Magazine. Department of the Army Public Affairs, 9325 Gunston Rd., Suite S108, Fort Belvoir, Virginia 22060-5548.

United States Army Combat Clothing and Equipment. Reprinted by George A. Peterson, National Capital Historical Sales, P.O. Box 605, Springfield, Virginia.

AAFES Army Military Clothing Catalog, 1994.

Rottman, Gordon, and Volstad, Ron. *Inside the US Army Today.* Osprey Publishing Limited, 1994

Weapon Systems. United States Army 1996, US Government Printing Office, 1996.

Army Green Book. Association of the United States Army 1989, 1990, 1991, 1992, 1993, 1994, 1995, 1996.

Army. Association of the United States Army.

Above: General Norman Schwarzkopf and Chairman of the Joint Chiefs of Staff Collin Powell listen to a briefing during the Persian Gulf War. General Powell wears the subdued insignia of rank, as well as subdued Combat Infantry Badge, Parachutist Qualification Badge and Pathfinders Badge. General Schwarzkopf wears the desert-pattern combat boot. Due to their rarity, these boots were seldom seen on the front lines during the Gulf War. (APA)

Right: During Operation Desert Shield a paratrooper from the 82nd Airborne Division takes a break to catch up on the news. He does not have an 82nd Airborne Insignia on his newly issued desert camouflage uniform, but his affiliation with the airborne forces is signified by the maroon beret he proudly wears. (APA)

Above: Infantry soldiers quickly deploy from the back of a Bradley Fighting Vehicle. The Bradley provides infantrymen with greater firepower and protection than the M113 Armored Personnel Carrier. The Bradley has a crew of three and can transport a six-man infantry squad. Its primary armament is a 25mm cannon. (APA)

Left: General Gordon R. Sullivan reviews the Commander in Chief's Guard with Secretary of the Army Michael P. Stone. General Sullivan is wearing the Class A uniform. He wears the service cap for field grade officers and above, signified by the gold braid on the visor. Among the decorations he wears on his uniform is the combat infantry badge. On his left breast he wears the Secretary of Defense Badge and the Joint Chiefs of Staff Badge. General Sullivan commanded the army during some of the most dramatic changes in its history. (APA)

Above right: An officer candidate school (OCS) cadet takes a compass bearing during a field exercise. He is wearing the lightweight, rip-stop, cotton battledress uniform (BDU). He has attached a flashlight to his ALICE gear. His cadet status is signified by the gold OCS insignia he wears on his jacket collar. The pouch on his right shoulder can be used to carry either a compass or, in this case, a field dressing. (APA)

Right: Happy to be home and enjoying the victory, this veteran of the Gulf War proudly shows 'Old Glory'. This G.I. wears the desert uniform and hat. In his left hand he carries his helmet with desert camouflage cover. He has attached a privately purchased flashlight to his ALICE equipment. (NGM)

Above: Heavily laden G.I.s take a break on an exercise. The men are all wearing the standard BDU uniform and helmet cover. SPC Miller has the standard subdued rank insignia attached to the front of his helmet. He has a well-stuffed ALICE knapsack on his back, which can carry all of a soldier's requirements for a lengthy field exercise. He has attached a 2-quart collapsible canteen to his pack. This is carried in addition to the standard canteen. To complete his load, Miller has strapped an ANPRC 119 radio to the top of his pack. (APA)

Left: Two officers wearing the evening mess dress. The mess dress is reserved for formal occasions. The officer on the left wears the mess dress for general officers. It can be distinguished by black velvet cuffs, black lapels and two gold stripes on the trouser legs. The light blue lapels of the officer on the right identify him as an infantry officer. Mess dress for officers below the rank of general can be signified by branch of service colours on the lapels. (NGM)

Above: Members of a National Guard transportation unit somewhere in the Persian Gulf. The build up of forces in the Middle East was sudden. Due to the large number of people called up for service in the Gulf, there was often a shortage of desert pattern BDUs. Many soldiers could be seen wearing the common woodland pattern camouflage. These soldiers reflect this variety. The soldier on the left wears the night-time desert BDU parka over desert pattern camouflage uniforms. The soldier on the right and kneeling in the right foreground wear the woodland pattern camouflage. (NGM)

Right: A close-up of a tank driver of the 24th Infantry Division based at Fort McPherson Georgia. He is wearing the DH-132 armoured crewman's helmet with sun, wind and dust goggles. The 24th Infantry Division was part of the XVIII Airborne Corps during the Gulf War and spearheaded the Desert Storm counter-offensive. Due to the force structure draw-downs, the 24th recently changed its designation to the 3rd Infantry Division. (APA)

A well-camouflaged member of the special forces, the famous 'Green Berets', during an exercise. He is wearing the light-weight BDU uniform with his special forces patch on the right shoulder. He has a well-filled ALICE pack which will support him for many days behind the lines. He is armed with an M16A1 rifle. (APA)

Above: During the long years of the Cold War, the Army had large numbers of soldiers, such as the ones pictured here during a 'Reforger' exercise in 1985, 'forward deployed' in Europe. These troops were prepared to halt an invasion of Western Europe by Warsaw Pact forces. Today, most of these troops have returned from Europe. (APA)

Below: A G.I. takes aim with his M16A2 rifle. He has a blank adapter attached to the muzzle of his rifle. He is wearing the daytime desert camouflage BDUs, known by G.I.s as 'chocolate chips'. He wears the neckerchief, man's cotton, knitted around his neck to absorb sweat and reduce chafing. (APA)

A new recruit who has just received his first clothing issue is escorted from the quartermaster by a DI. Both men wear the cotton and nylon uniform, battledress, temperate zone, in woodland pattern camouflage. This is the standard uniform of the army and is worn in the field and in garrison. (APA)

Right: A close-up of a colonel in the 7th Infantry Division illustrates the new GORTEX cold-weather parka. This jacket is part of the extended cold-weather clothing system (ECWCS) that began to reach soldiers in the field in the mid-1980s. The colonel has completely covered his Kevlar helmet with scrim obtained from old BDU uniforms. (APA)

Below: Today, G.I.s are deployed around the world in a wide variety of missions. Among the many new roles that the G.I. finds himself in is that of a United Nations peace-keeper. Here, two members of a U.S.-manned United Nations observer team discuss the elections with a member of the Haitian police. The men are wearing light blue baseball caps to signify that they are serving as part of the United Nations. American soldiers can also be seen wearing the blue beret in Macedonia, Turkey and elsewhere. (NGM)

Opposite page: Members of the Commander in Chief's Guard parade at a ceremony in Washington, D.C. The Guard is a component of the 3rd Infantry Regiment, the 'Old Guard'. The Commander in Chief's Guard wears uniforms and uses the drill of the continental army. The 3rd Infantry performs ceremonial functions throughout the Washington area, including providing the Guard for the Tomb of the Unknown Soldier at Arlington Cemetery. Membership in the Old Guard is considered to be a great honour and only the most competent soldiers are part of its ranks. (APA)

Right: During Operation Desert Storm an SGT takes a break to smoke his pipe. He is wearing the daytime desert camouflage uniform with green subdued insignia taken from the woodland pattern uniform. To shade himself from the sun he wears the desert pattern 'Boonie Hat'. Many examples of this hat can be seen where the owner had a description of his service in the Gulf embroidered into it, much as an earlier generation of G.I.s did in Vietnam. (APA)

Below: A scene familiar to any veteran G.I. A Drill Instructor (DI) at Fort Campbell, Kentucky 'instructs' a new recruit. The symbol of the DI is the hat, drill sergeant, male, enlisted, more commonly referred to as the 'Smokey the Bear' hat. The recruit can be identified by the plain helmet liner from the old M1 helmet being worn, and also the look of nervousness on his face. (APA)

Above: Two Military Police (MP) Women discuss their tour in Germany. Both women wear the woodland pattern BDU uniform. The MP on the left has draped her GORTEX parka over her right arm. The MP on the right wears an MP brassard attached to her left shoulder. In the field this brassard would be subdued. Under her jacket she wears the polypropylene cold-weather shirt. This shirt is the first layer of the extreme cold-weather clothing system (ECWCS). (NGM)

Left: Lieutenant Colonel Dan Drasheff visits his son, Staff Sergeant Don Drasheff, Jr. Both men are members of the 20th Special Forces Group. Drasheff, Jr. is wearing the Individual Integrated Fighting System Tactical Load Bearing Vest. This equipment is beginning to replace the ALICE equipment as the standard load-bearing equipment for the army. His father wears the famous green beret with rank insignia attached. On his jacket he wears the wings for master parachutist and pathfinder. The 20th Special Forces Group was deployed to Haiti. (NGM)

Right: Major Crawford is wearing the Kevlar helmet with camouflage cover. He has sewn his rank insignia to the front of his helmet. The Kevlar helmet, nicknamed the 'Fritz' helmet, is a component of the Personal Armor System for Ground Troops (PASGT). It began to be issued to troops in the field in the late 1970s and has now replaced the M1C helmet. (APA)

Left: The crew of a TPQ-36 radar set-up at the Turkish fort outside Sarajevo, Bosnia. The TPQ-36 is an advanced radar system that can track and position incoming artillery rounds almost immediately. This has proven to be very valuable as the IFOR forces in Bosnia try to track down weapons being used by the warring factions. Due to the dangerous situation facing U.S. soldiers in Bosnia, all members of the crew wear PASGT helmet and flak vest. (NGM)

Left: American soldiers pass through a simulated United Nations checkpoint at the Hoenfels training centre, Germany. Prior to deployment to Bosnia, soldiers of the 1st Armored Division went through an intensive training period to prepare for their peace-keeping duties in Bosnia. These operations other than war (OOTW), often under UN auspices, will become an increasingly common mission for G.I.s. (NGM)

Above: A smiling drill instructor (DI) wears the famous 'Smokey the Bear' hat. The roundel on the front of his hat is for enlisted personnel. Under the DI's gentle care, a volunteer will undergo an eight-week basic training programme. This programme will emphasise basic military skills such as drill and ceremony, physical fitness and weapons familiarisation. These first eight weeks will convert a civilian recruit into a soldier. (APA)

Right: Despite the impersonal nature of the modern battlefield, there are still times when a soldier will have to close with the enemy. Pugil stick training is used by the Army as a means of building aggressiveness in its recruits. Because of the heat of Fort McClellan, Alabama, where this training is taking place, both men wear the olive green (OG) 109 cotton undershirt under their protective equipment. Their rolled-up trousers give a good view of the black leather combat boots. (APA)

Above: After completion of basic training, soldiers are sent to Advanced Individual Training (AIT). These advanced schools teach the specific military skills that the soldier willl use in the service. This is where the soldier will acquire a specific military occupational specialty (MOS) that he or she will practise while in the service. One of the tougher advanced schools is the Air Assault School. Here, students learn that there is much more to school than jumping out of helicopters. (APA)

Left: Some things remain the same in all armies at all times. Here, two recruits have been assigned to Kitchen Police (KP) duty. They are wearing a disposable kitchen hat and apron over their BDU uniform. (APA)

Right: Somewhere in the Persian Gulf a soldier takes some time to keep in shape using improvised exercise equipment. The weight-lifter has taken off his BDU jacket and is wearing an OG 109 cotton undershirt. Due to the fear of chemical use by the Iraqis, this soldier keeps his M17A2 mask at the ready. (APA)

Below: Students at Air Assault School hone their physical skills. These students are doing chin-ups with full packs. They are wearing the old M1C-pattern helmet with identification numbers during their training. The packs they are wearing are a component of the All Purpose Lightweight Individual Carrying Equipment (ALICE). A fully loaded pack can carry approximately 50 lbs of equipment. For heavier loads, the pack can be attached to a rigid aluminium frame. (APA)

Soldiers of the 20th Engineer Brigade Cruise across the desert in an M1A1 Abrams Tank that they have named 'Final Option'. The M1A1 proved to be one of the great success stories of the Persian Gulf War. Its 120mm gun was able to dominate the Russian-built T-72 tank. Only four Abrams were lost to enemy action during the course of the war. (APA)

Left: Somewhere in the Persian Gulf a member of the 1267th Medical Company points to his home-town. Unofficial signposts such as this have been a feature of American military encampments throughout history. Note the one sign pointing straight down. (NGM)

Right: A soldier on guard duty during Operation Desert Storm. Due to the shortage of the desert camouflage uniform, the sentry is wearing the standard woodland pattern camouflage BDU uniform and helmet cover underneath her desert nighttime camouflage parka. This parka is light green with a dark green grid pattern and is designed to lessen the effects of the enemy's night vision equipment. (NGM)

Right: A member of the 1221st Transportation Unit proudly displays a good luck blanket sent by Girl Scouts back home. Such messages from home greatly improved the morale and fighting effectiveness of the troops deployed to the Persian Gulf. The sergeant is wearing a Desert Camouflage Jacket and 'Boonie' hat. (NGM)

Left: An MP during the Gulf War is wearing a tan MP brassard attached to his woodland camouflage jacket. Of special interest are the Arabic characters written on the armband. These characters were utilised to ease identification of the MPs by the many Arab soldiers of the coalition forces aligned against Saddam Hussein. (NGM)

Left: A fire team and its squad leader of the 101st Airborne (Air Assault) Division conduct a patrol of enemy positions. The men all wear the daytime desert camouflage uniform and lightweight jungle boots. The two men in the foreground have a desert field-pack cover. This cover is designed to camouflage the olive-green ALICE equipment. While many soldiers had this camouflage cover during the war, it was not universally seen, as demonstrated by the other members of this patrol. (APA)

Above: A soldier takes a breather from the high temperatures and tension. Over his desert BDU uniform the soldier wears the Personal Armor System for Ground Troops (PASGT) flak vest. This vest weighs 3.8 kilograms and is intended to reduce wounds caused by shell fragments and small arms ammunition. A cover made of daytime desert camouflage material is available, but was seldom seen in the desert. Of special interest are the men standing behind this soldier who are all wearing the woodland pattern uniform. (APA)

Left: A XVII Airborne Corps soldier starts out on a patrol. He is wearing the ALICE equipment. Around his neck he carries a thermal imaging system that will be used to spot enemy movement at night. Over his right shoulder he carries the 2 quart collapsible canteen in a tan colour. He is wearing the standard black leather combat boots. (APA)

Above: Paratroopers of a four-man fire team practise advance to contact drill in the months preceding the start of Operation Desert Storm. The G.I.s have all tied privately acquired kerchiefs around their necks. The soldier on the right carries the M-60 machine gun. The 7.62mm M60 has been the squad automatic weapon (SAW) since the Vietnam War. (APA)

Below: A 5th Special Forces soldier test-fires his Mk-19 40mm automatic grenade launcher. The MK-19 is a 72 lb weapon that can throw shells at targets up to 2000 metres away. The MK-19 is slowly replacing the M2 heavy machine gun in many units. It can be carried individually or mounted on a variety of chassis. (APA)

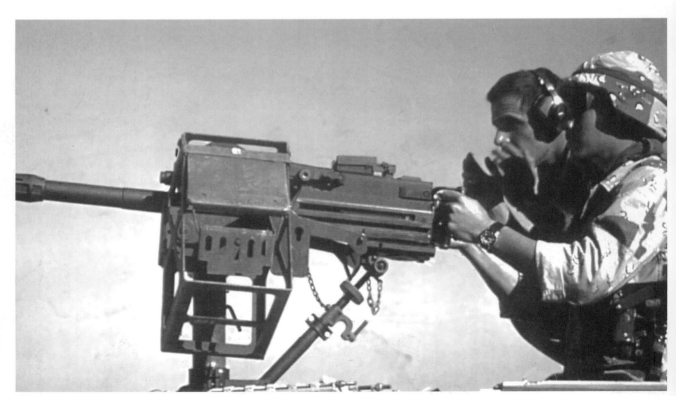

Above: Captain Morris briefs soldiers of D Company, 25th Signal Battalion. While most of the men are wearing the daytime desert camouflage uniform, some of Morris's men wear woodland pattern camouflage. Due to the suddenness and size of the build-up for the Gulf War, there was a shortage of the desert uniforms. The woodland pattern camouflage was commonly seen in the desert. Morris also wears the lightweight jungle boot. (NGM)

Below: A squad leader signals his men forward. This sergeant has been able to obtain the cover for his flak jacket. He has also attached a bayonet to the end of his M16A2 rifle. The M16A2 is the latest version of this rifle and is slowly replacing earlier M16A1 models. (APA)

Left: Colonel Zanini addresses the men of the 1st Armored Division. Zanini and his men have deployed to the Persian Gulf from Germany. This may explain why they are all wearing woodland pattern equipment. The colonel has a privately procured pen-holder attached to his shoulder holster. He has obtained a World War Two era .45 calibre ammunition pouch that he has attached to the right side of his belt. Zanini wears the patch of the 2nd Armored 'Hell on Wheels' Division on his right shoulder. This indicates prior service with that unit. (APA)

Right: The desert proved to be very harsh on weapons and equipment. Here, a soldier of the XVIII Airborne Corps checks his M16A2 for problems. The A2 is an 8.9 lb weapon that fires 5.56mm ammunition. This ammunition is NATO standard. It is fired in three-round controlled bursts. Just visible in the pack behind him is the night-time desert camouflage parka. (APA)

Below: The Corps of Cadets on parade at the U.S. Military Academy at West Point. They are wearing a uniform that has remained virtually unchanged since the academy was founded. These cadets have met the rigid academic requirements to enter the academy. After a rigorous four-year programme, graduates are commissioned as second lieutenants in the Army. The Army's senior leadership have historically been graduates of West Point. (APA)

Above: Eskimo Scouts prepare for the inaugural parade of President Clinton. The Eskimo Scouts are comprised principally of native Americans. The unit is an element of the Alaska National Guard. It has served as the guardian of America's northernmost state since World War Two. These scouts all wear the White Arctic Snow Camouflage parka and trousers. This camouflage clothing is worn over standard cold-weather clothing. On its own, the snow camouflage has no insulating properties. (NGM)

Right: An Alaska Scout during an exercise. He wears the snow camouflage trousers and an earlier pattern olive-green field jacket. His cold-weather headgear is unique to the Scouts. He is armed with an M16 rifle and his equipment is the earlier cotton webbing version of the ALICE gear; modern versions of this equipment are made in nylon. (NGM)

Above: Alaska Scouts preparing to go out on patrol. They all wear the extreme cold-weather parka with hood underneath their snow camouflage. They are also wearing the extreme cold-weather mittens with camouflage cover. Of special interest are the snowmobiles that have been camouflaged in white paint. The snowmobiles are necessary for the Scouts to traverse the great distances they are responsible for in Alaska. (NGM)

Left: A private of the 2nd Infantry Division in Korea takes a breather. The 2nd Infantry Division has been stationed in Korea since the Korean War. It is there to ensure the integrity of the border between North and South Korea. Duty on the Korean border has proven to be physically and mentally demanding, as the soldiers watch over one of the last vestiges of the Cold War. The soldier wears the extreme cold-weather parka and a Kevlar helmet. (APA)

Opposite page, top: During a training exercise a soldier takes aim with his M16A2. On his helmet is attached the XM60 Multiple Integrated Laser Engagement System (MILES). MILES equipment is an advanced laser detection system that is used in training exercises. The detection devices on the equipment record when a hit has been scored by emitting a load beeping noise which can only be turned off by an umpire. This has greatly enhanced the realism of training exercises. (APA)

Opposite page, bottom: Members of the 28th Infantry Division conduct a patrol during a training exercise. All the men are wearing the standard BDU uniform and Kevlar helmet. Their medium ALICE packs seem to be full, indicating that they are on an extended field exercise. The 28th Division is the oldest division in the Army and served with great distinction in both World Wars. (NGM)

Right: A before and after shot of an Army sniper. The soldier kneeling in the foreground wears the standard BDU uniform and an M43 field cap. The soldier standing in the background wears a ghillie suit. Each ghillie suit is individually made out of burlap and camouflage netting. Normally, snipers are armed with the M-24 bolt action rifle, not the M16 as pictured here. (APA)

Opposite page, top: An infantryman of the 28th Division takes in his surroundings during a patrol. His unit is identified by the black patch on his left shoulder. This is a subdued version of the 28th's patch. This patch is officially red. All soldiers wear subdued patches on their BDU uniforms, which eliminates the need to remove patches in the field. (NGM)

Opposite page, bottom: Two infantry companies are lined up for inspection. The officers stand in front of each company. Also in front of each company is its guidon. This identifies the unit's battalion number and company letter. The guidon also features the symbol of each branch, eg crossed rifles for infantry. These guidons designate a company's place in formation and also serve to build esprit de corps within a company. (APA)

Above: An artillery soldier guards his battery's perimeter with a .50 calibre machine gun. The .50 calibre, now designated as the M2, has been in service since World War Two. The artilleryman is attached to a self-propelled gun. This can be determined because he is wearing the armoured crewman's coveralls and not the BDU uniform. (APA)

Right: Among the many new missions that the G.I. faces today is aid to civil authorities. In this photograph a soldier from the 9th Infantry Division is assisting the U.S. Forestry Service in fighting a forest fire. The soldier wears the forestry service fire-fighting uniform, but has attached his military rank to the collar of his jacket to identify the fact that he is in the military. (APA)

Left: Staff Sergeant Jill Henderson was the 1993 Drill Sergeant of the year. Henderson is seated in front of a statue of Athena, the Greek goddess of war. Athena was the symbol of the Women's Army Corps (WAC) until it was disbanded as a separate branch in the 1970s. Her position as a drill instructor is signified by the hat she wears – unique to female drill instructors. (APA)

Below: The Sherpa is one of the few fixed wing aircraft that is an Army asset. The Sherpa is used as a short-distance shuttle aircraft that can carry personnel or equipment. It is used extensively by the Puerto Rico National Guard. (NGM)

Right: With the increased reliance on helicopter lift of large numbers of troops, as demonstrated by the XVII Airborne Corps during the Persian Gulf War, the Army now has its own air traffic controllers. These soldiers are responsible for ensuring the safe landing of many helicopters on to a landing zone. The controller wears a pullover jersey with a blaze orange front. Due to the amount of debris tossed into the air by the chopper's blades, this soldier wears a pair of safety glasses. (APA)

Below: A jump master checks to see that everything is in order before a jump. The paratrooper being inspected wears the old-pattern olive-green fatigues. The trooper also wears the Kevlar helmet with cover. Although the Kevlar's suspension system is the same for both infantry and paratrooper models, there is additional padding that paratroopers can insert into their helmets for added protection. (APA)

Opposite page, top An AH-15 Cobra Attack Helicopter can carry eight TOW missiles, 750 rounds of 20mm cannon ammunition and 76 2.75-inch rockets. It uses this formidable array of weaponry in its anti-armour attack role. It is also used to provide escort to friendly armour columns and reconnaissance. The Cobra is slowly being replaced by the Apache helicopter, but extension programmes will keep it in the fleet for some time. (APA)

Above: Stand up and hook up! Soldiers of the 82nd prepare to jump from a C-130 Aircraft. These troopers wear the woodland pattern uniform and Kevlar helmet. Their main 'chute is rectangular, this aids manoeuvrability during the descent and reduces the risk of accidents. (APA)

Left: A group of Air Assault soldiers prepare to load up. These soldiers specialise in rapid insertion into the battle area. The 101st Airborne (Air Assault) are among those troops who specialise in this sort of warfare. The 101st is now officially an Air Assault Division and carries the word 'airborne' in its title as an honorary designation. (APA)

Left: A variant of the M113 APC, this is a M901/ITV (Improved TOW Vehicle) mounting a TOW anti-tank missile system. TOW is an acronym for Tube-launched, Optically-tracked, Wire-guided. The missile has a range of nearly 4km and with the lastest warhead is capable of knocking out any of the current main battle tanks. (APA)

Opposite page, bottom: The Multiple Launch Rocket System was one of the 'Big Five' during Operation Desert Storm. This vehicle can travel 480 miles at speeds of up to 40 mph. The Army plans to increase the number of these rocket systems as time and funds are available. The MLRS will become the primary counter-battery and fire-suppression weapon for the Army at the beginning of the 21st century. (APA)

Below: Infantry soldiers 'debus' from the back of an M113 while one of the vehicle's two crew members covers them with an M2 machine gun. All of the soldiers have blank adapters attached to their weapons and are wearing MILES gear. The soldier in the foreground has covered his helmet in the plastic scrim used to cover vehicles. The M113 APC, first used in the 1960s, was the standard APC for most of the Cold War. This versatile vehicle has undergone seven upgrades to keep it on par with other modern weapon systems. The last upgrade, the M113A3, can travel up to 300 miles at speeds of up to 42 mph. While its standard armament is the M2 machine gun, there are thirty-five other variants of the M113 that feature a wide variety of weapon platforms. (APA)

Opposite page, top: An MLRS gets ready to fire. This photograph clearly shows the twelve rocket tubes on the MLRS. Due to its mobility, just seconds after firing all of its tubes, the vehicle can exit an area. This mobility greatly enhances its survivability on the battlefield. (APA)

Opposite page, bottom: Soldiers of the 72nd Engineers test a mine-clearing rake – more commonly referred to as a 'plough' – that they have attached to a M-782 Combat Engineer Vehicle. The M-782 is a variant of the M60A1 tank, the Army's main battle tank prior to the introduction of the Abrams. This mine-clearing device was extremely valuable in clearing the numerous Iraqi minefields that were emplaced in Kuwait. (APA)

Right: During a prison disturbance in Ohio a National Guard soldier is called on to assist law enforcement authorities in defusing the situation. This soldier is wearing the M-69 body armour fragmentation vest, an earlier version of the PASGT. He is armed with a 12 gauge shotgun, which has been temporarily issued for this emergency by local law enforcement authorities. It is not a regularly issued firearm to military personnel. (NGM)

Below: Graduates of the U.S. Army War College pose for a photograph. These officers illustrate a wide variety of what is considered to be 'Class B' uniform. All of them wear the Class A army green trousers for officers and the shade 428 green shirt. Officers can be distinguished by the insignia worn on their epaulets. The officers in the front row are also wearing the men's and women's sweater black. These officers would all be in Class A uniform if they were to wear the same uniform with the jacket and black tie. (NGM)

Opposite page, top: Soldiers train for riot duty. These men have added a face shield to their Kevlar helmets for added protection. Soldiers are receiving extra training in civil disturbance scenarios. The Army is increasingly likely to deploy soldiers for operations of this type, as was evident in Haiti and Somalia as well as during the Los Angeles riots and Hurricane Andrew. (NGM)

Opposite page, bottom: A public affairs soldier of the *Talon* newspaper interviews a soldier in Bosnia. The *Talon* is the paper for members of Task Force Eagle. Despite his non-combatant role, this reporter wears the Kevlar helmet and flak vest, due to the dangerous conditions in Bosnia. He has sewn an American flag to his right shoulder to designate to the Bosnians that he is an American soldier and not a member of one of the various warring factions. This is the special 'reversed' flag with stars to the front, designed for wear on the right sleeve. (NGM)

Right: A female officer wearing the shade 428 green shirt for women. Her rank is indicated by the black slip-on insignia worn on her lapels. The black universal neck tab is worn by women in lieu of the tie. With this uniform she can wear either a skirt or slacks. All personnel, male and female, wear name-plates on the right breast of their Class A and B uniform. (NGM)

Below: A soldier breaks into a broad grin after he has been presented the Legion of Merit by the general on the left. All men wear the rip-stop BDU uniform. The general wears the pistol belt for general officers as part of his uniform. This black leather belt is unique to general officers. The tongue and wreath buckle features the coat of arms of the United States. The belt is only worn with the BDU uniform. (NGM)

Above: The Army's navy. To support the many rapid deployment contingencies that soldiers face today, the Army operates a small number of Landing Craft Marine (LCM). These vessels are manned by army personnel and work in conjunction with navy vessels. The LCM is a shallow draught vessel that can transport men and material on to a hostile shore. Some LCMs are equipped with M2 or M60 machine guns for defence. (NGM)

Left: Sergeant Naipo wears the shade 482 green shirt. His non-commissioned status is designated by his epaulets. Officers' epaulets have a band of gold braid on the end, enlisted do not. Just visible on the sergeant's left breast is the Army National Guard recruiting badge. (NGM)

Opposite page, top: An Army Chinook helicopter delivers communications equipment to one of Iceland's mountain rescue teams. The Chinook is a medium lift helicopter that can transport forty-four fully equipped soldiers up to 1260 miles. The MH-47E is a variant of the Chinook that is being employed by U.S. Special Operations Command (USSOCOM). The MH-47E features two 7.62mm miniguns for added firepower. (NGM)

Opposite page, bottom: Even in a hostile environment nature calls. These soldiers are wearing the hoods and mask of the chemical protective suit. These men are considered to be in a mission-orientated protective posture (MOPP) 1, comprising the chemical mask and hood. MOPP 2 adds gloves and MOPP 3 includes the full suit that provides protection against nuclear, biological and chemical (NBC) contaminants. (NGM)

Left: Sergeant Dahlvig sits for an official photograph. He is in Class A uniform for enlisted personnel. On his jacket lapels are his branch of service insignia, in this case, the Adjutant's General Corps. He has the National Guard Recruiter's badge on his left breast and Joint Chiefs of Staff badge on his right breast. Also on his right breast, above his name-plate, is a branch of service insignia. (NGM)

Below: A quarter-ton Jeep on the move. These MPs are taking part in a training exercise prior to Operation Just Cause. This was the last major military operation to utilise the M151, the final variant of the immortal Jeep. The HMMWV has now totally replaced the Jeep and other small utility vehicles. (NGM)

Opposite page, top: Light reconnaissance vehicles such as this one are sometimes utilised by special forces units. Navy SEALS used vehicles like this during many of their missions behind Iraqi lines prior to the start of the ground phase of Operation Desert Storm. Such vehicles have generally been replaced as more and more variants of the versatile HMMWV are introduced. (APA)

Opposite page, bottom: Members of the 82nd Airborne discuss their position with an officer during a deployment to Honduras. The Army maintains close ties with many Latin American countries and regularly participates in training exercises in this part of the world. The officer kneeling on the left has chosen to wear the SRU-21/P survival vest instead of ALICE gear. The SRU vest is normally worn by aviators. (APA)

Left: A Palletised Load System (PLS) prime mover. This truck is carrying replacement tubes for an MLRS. The 16.5 ton PLS has a range of 255 miles. The vehicle can be modified to carry a variety of loads. The truck is interoperable with comparable French, German and British systems. The truck is equipped to operate in a fully tactical environment. (APA)

Opposite page, bottom: In the Saudi Desert, soldiers of the 101st Airborne fire their M119A1 105mm howitzer on enemy positions. The M1191 is used by airborne, air assault and light infantry divisions in lieu of the much heavier M109 self-propelled gun. It can be towed on the battlefield by an HMMWV or airlifted by a Black Hawk helicopter. (APA)

Below: A crew of an M113 camouflage their vehicle. They are using plastic camouflage net that is supplied in a variety of sizes and can be found on most vehicles in a variety of environments. This netting is also used by soldiers to break up the outline of helmets and ghillie suits. The netting comes in a variety of colours. (APA)

Left: Officers of the 7th Infantry Division coordinate their plans. Both men are wearing scrim-covered helmets and nylon ALICE equipment. Nowhere are there any visible signs of rank on either officer. (APA)

Right: Sergeant Ray Gonzales takes a break from training at Fort Polk, Louisiana. He is wearing a typical field uniform and has concealed the outline of his helmet with a healthy amount of scrim. The camouflage on his helmet is made up of pieces of old camouflage clothing. (APA)

Below: A soldier of the 300th Service and Supply Battalion, equipped with an M16A2 rifle. For purposes of a training exercise, he has attached a blank adaptor to the muzzle of his rifle. (NGM)

Opposite page, top: Two MPs confer during exercises in Louisiana. Both men are wearing the XM60 MILES gear. This equipment is used during training exercises and, with the help of lasers mounted on participants' weapons, accurately registers 'hits'. The soldier on the left has wrapped his trousers in duck tape to prevent insects from crawling up his legs. (NGM)

Opposite page, bottom: Two Army CH-47 Chinook helicopter crewmen participate in Operation Northern Neighbor at Isafjordur, Iceland. The two men are wearing the Lightweight Flyer's Jacket over their aviators' coveralls. Both men are wearing the SPH-4 Flyer's Helmet. (NGM)

Below: An Army Public Affairs soldier prepares to conduct an interview in Bosnia. Due to the dangerous conditions in Bosnia, the sergeant is wearing his fragmentation vest and Kevlar helmet. Army Public Affairs personnel regularly cover stories on the missions and deployments of the Army in the field. (NGM)

Opposite page: A Military Policeman takes aim with his M9 9mm pistol. This semi-automatic, double action pistol has replaced the venerable M1911A1 pistol as the standard side-arm of the Army. It is carried by crew-served weapon crewmen, Military Police personnel and aviators. (NGM)

Above: Military Policeman SPC Paul A. Bierod works with a Panamanian Police officer in Panama. Bierod is wearing the summer weight 'rip-stop' BDUs . Note ear-plugs affixed to the collar of his jacket. (NGM)

Below: SPC Sergie Chukwak gently places a Claymore anti-personnel mine into position. This battery-operated mine has proved to be highly effective against enemy ground personnel, and has been part of the American soldier's arsenal since the Vietnam War. (NGM)

Opposite page, top: An infantry-man leans back and prepares to release a grenade while an instructor looks on. Despite the digitised nature of the modern battlefield, even now there are times when the infantryman must get 'up-close', so skills such as the grenade are still taught. (NGM)

Opposite page, bottom: The G.I. of today must be prepared for deployment anywhere in the world and be ready to perform in a wide variety of environments. Here soldiers train for operations in snow and cold, and are wearing the cold-dry uniform, which is comprised of several layers of clothing designed to ensure warmth. They are also wearing the insulated cold-weather boot, lined with three layers of wool fleece. (NGM)

Right: PFC Patricia Villanueva plays with some Panamanian children. The Army is involved with a number of missions in Central and South America that are designed to strengthen relations between the United States and its Latin American neighbours. Villanueva wears the poplin hot-weather uniform. This lightweight uniform is made in wind-resistant 'rip-stop' cotton. (NGM)

Opposite page: While undergoing Jungle Training in Panama, SGT Owen Bower has reversed his battledress jacket to signify his participation as an opposing forces 'OPFOR' member. He is armed with the M16A2 rifle, carried on an improvised sling. (NGM)

Above: A camouflaged SPC Bill Hecksel advances on his opposition during a training exercise. Hecksel is armed with an M16A1 with an attached M203 grenade launcher. The launcher, which is effective out to 350 metres, adds a tremendous amount of firepower to the infantry squad. (NGM)

Opposite page, top: A soldier undergoing Jungle Training at Fort Sherman, Panama takes a break to rest his feet. He has taken off his lightweight combat boots. These are the latest version of the famous 'Jungle Boot', but are all black and feature 'speed lace' hooks. (NGM)

Opposite page, bottom Two long-service Army National Guard helicopter pilots stand in front of their chopper. They are wearing the aviation crewman nomex coveralls. These fire-retardant coveralls are worn by all Army aviators. Both pilots have leather name-tags affixed to their left breast and unit-made patches attached to the right. (NGM)

Above: Members of the 1st Battalion 20th Special Forces Group are training at the MOUT site at Fort Bragg, North Carolina before their deployment to Haiti. Of special interest is the medic's bag on the back of the soldier 'covering' the prisoners with his M16 rifle. (NGM)

Right: Engineers somewhere in U.S. Army Southern Command (SOUTHCOM) are engaged in a bridge-building exercise. The two soldiers in the front are wearing 'Boonie' hats and grey army physical training (PT) shorts. They all wear privately purchased running shoes. The extreme temperatures of Central America no doubt necessitated this extremely casual uniform. (NGM)

Left: A very wet lieutenant returns from an exercise. He is wearing the GORTEX cold-weather jacket. GORTEX clothing has only recently entered the Army's inventory. Attached to the lieutenant's ALICE load-bearing equipment are a pair of ear-plugs carried in their plastic container and a pen flashlight. (APA)

Right: Under the watchful eye of an NCO, a soldier prepares to take aim with a Stinger missile. The Stinger Anti-Aircraft missile is a single-shot weapon that has replaced the M41 rocket system. After firing, the launch tube is discarded. (NGM)

Below: CPT Eric Stevenson guides his Bradley fighting vehicle back from an exercise. The photograph is a good illustration of the DH-132 Armored Vehicle Crewman's helmet. Stevenson is also wearing the Combat Vehicle Crewman coveralls. (NGM)

Opposite page: Three mechanics work on the engine of a Bradley fighting vehicle. The two mechanics on the left are wearing mechanics' coveralls. These olive-drab coveralls are worn in addition to BDU uniforms by mechanics. (NGM)

Above: Army journalist SPC Janis Tanimoto introduces herself to some of the local population of Guatemala. She is wearing summer weight BDU uniform and 'Boonie' hat. (NGM)

Left: This Army band is leading a parade in the Philippines celebrating the 50th anniversary of the Philippines' liberation from the Japanese. They are all wearing the Class B uniform, frequently worn in tropical climates because there is no longer a khaki dress uniform. (NGM)

Above: The TOW mounted on a Hummer. This is just another variant of the HMMWV that provides increased firepower to the infantry soldiers it supports. (APA)

Opposite page, top: An infantryman takes a break after an encounter with OPFOR forces. He is wearing the olive green rain suit. He has MILES gear attached to his helmet. He is sitting next to an anti-tank missile. (NGM)

Left: A Vehicle crewman surveys the terrain with his M22 binoculars. These binoculars are shielded against the effects of enemy lasers. His M60 has a blank adaptor attached, and a box of blank rounds is visible in the ammunition tray on the side of the gun mount. (NGM)

Right: TOW missile launcher is mounted on top of an M113. The TOW missile has been produced in five variants since 1970. It is a long-range heavy anti-tank missile with a thermal imaging system that allows the missile to be fired at night. Note how the mount for the M2 machine gun can fold down to allow the TOW to be traversed. (NGM)

Opposite page, bottom: The AN/PVS-7 night-vision goggles are provided to individual soldiers. Other variants are mounted on vehicles, or incorporated into gunsights. The night-vision equipment currently employed by the Army has been one of the principal reasons that the American soldier has been able to dominate the modern battlefield, as he did during the Persian Gulf War. This is a technology that will become increasingly important to the G.I. of the 21st century. The night-vision goggles are being worn in conjunction with a Kevlar helmet without the cover. Most Kevlar helmets are finished in plain olive-drab and are not camouflaged as this one has been. (APA)

Below: A soldier of the 502nd Infantry Regiment, 101st Airborne Division, scans the Sinai. This soldier is part of the Multi-National Force Observers (MFO). He wears the distinctive burnt orange beret of this unit. On his right shoulder is the MFO patch: a dove holding an olive branch on a burnt orange background. He also wears an American flag to identify himself as part of the multi-national contingent. (APA)

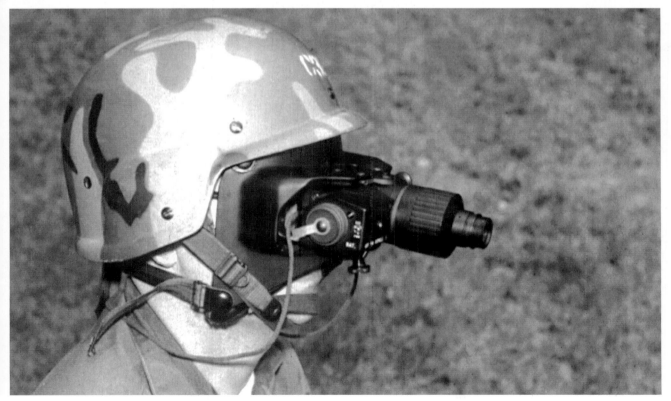

Above: Soldiers of the MFO discuss the mission; four of the five men wear the new daytime desert BDU uniform, which has deleted the darker brown and black shades from the original uniform. This can be compared with that of the soldier who is seated second from the left who wears the original daytime desert camouflage uniform. All the men wear the lightweight combat boot in a 'natural' or sand colour. Notice, however, that the subdued patches are still in green and black. Some versions of the subdued patches have been produced in tan and brown to match the uniform better, but these have not been widely circulated. (NGM)

Opposite page and right: Members of an Opposition Forces (OPFOR) unit prepare to go out on an exercise. The OPFOR claims to be the best Soviet unit in the American Army, training and using Soviet-style tactics. Its equipment is either Soviet or modified American. Here, members of OPFOR wear woodland-pattern BDU trousers and the old-style green fatigue jacket. The patch on the right shoulder is the symbol of OPFOR. All the men are wearing MILES gear. (NGM)

Two soldiers fire a Dragon anti-tank missile. This is a heavy anti-tank weapon that greatly enhances the firepower of the infantry. The Dragon is a single-shot, man-portable weapon. The tube is discarded after firing. (APA)

INDEX